W9-AFS-648

Class Trip
NEW YORK CITY

Elizabeth Scholl

Mitchell Lane
PUBLISHERS

P.O. Box 196
Hockessin, Delaware 19707
Visit us on the web: www.mitchelllane.com
Comments? email us: mitchelllane@mitchelllane.com

Mitchell Lane
PUBLISHERS

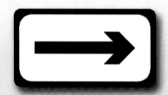

Boston • **New York City**
Philadelphia • San Antonio • San Diego
Washington, D.C.

Printing   1   2   3   4   5   6   7   8   9

Library of Congress
Cataloging-in-Publication Data
Scholl, Elizabeth J.
  Class trip New York City / by Elizabeth Scholl.
    p. cm. — (A Robbie reader—class trip)
  Includes bibliographical references and index.
  ISBN 978-1-58415-808-0 (library bound)
  1. New York (N.Y.)—Juvenile literature. 2. New York (N.Y.)—Description and travel—Juvenile literature. I. Title. II. Title: New York City.
  F128.33.S36 2009
  974.7'1—dc22

                              2009001110

                                      PLB

CONTENTS

NEW YORK CITY

The Statue of Liberty stands in New York Harbor. She is 305 feet tall and weighs over 300,000 pounds. Her sandals are 25 feet long. In women's shoe sizes, Lady Liberty would wear a size 879. *Right: The Mets' Home Run Apple*

Chapter 1

Something Different

It was Monday morning. As the school bell rang, we filed in and sat down. The classroom's two white mice, Harry and Tonto, scampered through the tube in their cage, then jumped onto their play wheel, running around and around. Books were stacked neatly on the back ledge. Yep, things were always pretty much the same at Hillsdale Elementary.

The only difference today was the two large maps pinned to the bulletin board. The old-looking one said *New Amsterdam.* The other showed New York City. I had heard of New York City, but where was New Amsterdam?

After attendance was taken and the mice were fed, Ms. Harrington asked us to guess why the maps were there. Several hands shot up. Ms. Harrington called on Bonnie. "Are we going to study New York and Amsterdam?" Bonnie asked. "Amsterdam is in the Netherlands."

"Right, Bonnie. Amsterdam is in the Netherlands, which is in Europe. And we are going to study New

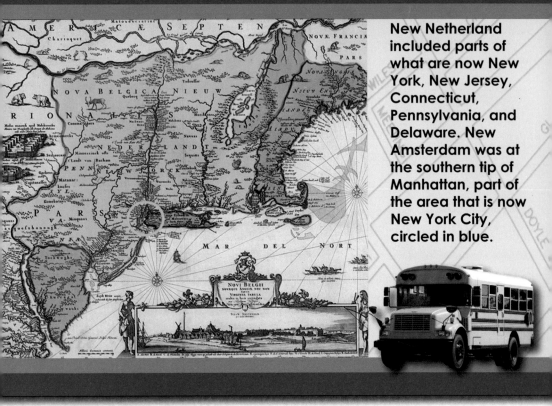

New Netherland included parts of what are now New York, New Jersey, Connecticut, Pennsylvania, and Delaware. New Amsterdam was at the southern tip of Manhattan, part of the area that is now New York City, circled in blue.

York City. Why would we study Amsterdam and New York City together?" Ms. Harrington asked. "Marcus?"

"Well, maybe people from Amsterdam traveled to New York a long time ago?" Marcus guessed.

"Correct, Marcus! Dutch explorers did travel to New York City in the 1600s. Now look closely at the older map. There is a clue that will help you figure out something about the map."

I had an idea, and raised my hand. "Yes, Laurel?" Ms. Harrington said.

"It says *Manahatta Island* on the New Amsterdam map. My cousin lives in part of New York City called Manhattan. Is New Amsterdam an old name for New York City?" I asked.

"Good thinking, Laurel!" Ms. Harrington exclaimed. "Now, who can guess why it was called New Amsterdam? Justin?"

"Was New York owned by Amsterdam?" Justin asked.

"Very good, Justin," Ms. Harrington said. "In the 1600s, the Dutch came to the island that is now Manhattan. They called it *Manahatta*, an Indian word for 'hilly island.' The **Lenape** Indians living there traded in furs, which were valuable in the Netherlands and in other places. They traded them with the Dutch for tools, sewing items, and cloth. By 1635, the Dutch colonists began building a village across the harbor. They called it Breuckelen, which today is Brooklyn.

She walked over to the the other map. "If you look at the newer map, you can see Manhattan, Brooklyn,

Peter Stuyvesant was the Director General of New Amsterdam from 1647 until the British takeover in 1664. He had a peg leg, which replaced a leg crushed by a cannonball in battle. Stuyvesant was famous for declaring to colonists, "I will govern you as a father his children." An apartment complex called Stuyvesant Town in downtown Manhattan stands on what was once Peter Stuyvesant's farm. Stuyvesant High School is also named for him.

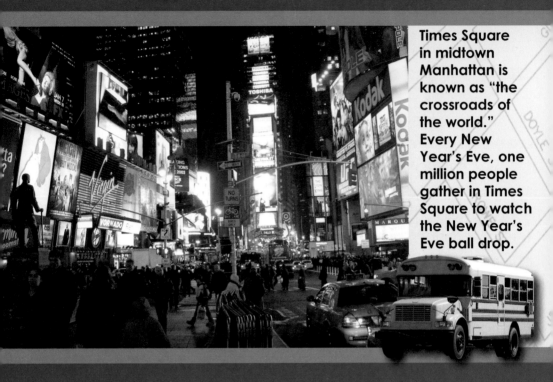

Times Square in midtown Manhattan is known as "the crossroads of the world." Every New Year's Eve, one million people gather in Times Square to watch the New Year's Eve ball drop.

and the three other areas, called **boroughs**, of New York City. They are the Bronx, Staten Island, and Queens. The Dutch called their settlement New Amsterdam, after the largest city in the Netherlands.

"So," Ms. Harrington continued, "we are going to learn about the history of New York City, as well as its geography, plants, and animals. We will also learn about the people and places there. What do you think would be the best way to learn about New York City?"

"We could watch a movie about New York," Marta suggested.

"That's a good idea, Marta. We actually will be watching several films about New York City." That didn't sound too bad to me. Movies were more interesting than our social studies book. "Anyone else?" Ms. Harrington asked. "Michael?"

"We could do a group project where each group studies a different part of the city, and then presents their project to the class," Michael said. That might be okay, I thought, but it would depend on who was in my group.

"I have a great idea!" shouted Alexis. "We could take a class trip to New York City! Then we would really be able to learn about it!"

Just as I was thinking that Alexis's idea was crazy, Ms. Harrington exclaimed, "You guessed my surprise, Alexis! Next week, we'll be spending a day in New York City. I'll give you a tour, since I used to live there."

The class broke out into a loud cheer. We'd been on school trips before, but never one like this! Wow, everything *wasn't* always the same at school. This was going to be awesome.

Everyone started asking questions about New York City. "How tall is the Empire State Building?" "How many people live in New York City?" "Are there any animals there?"

"Well, I'm glad you are all so interested in New York City," Ms. Harrington said. "Let's start finding out about it. Our trip is not until next week, and in the meantime, we'll begin by learning some history of the city."

A street performer

9

NEW YORK CITY

Built between the Hudson and East rivers, Manhattan island is only 2.3 miles across at its widest point. Right: The Empire State Building lit up at dusk

Chapter 2

From New Amsterdam to Greater New York

In 1609, English explorer Henry Hudson arrived in New York Harbor. He was looking for the **Northwest Passage**, a shortcut to Asia. The Lenape people who lived in the area offered him gifts of Indian wheat and tobacco.

Hudson told the Dutch about the riches of the "New World." The first settlers sent to Manhattan by the **Dutch West India Company** didn't pay the Lenape for the land. In 1624, Peter Minuit arrived and was chosen as the leader of the settlement. He gave the Lenapes two boxes of goods containing items such as hatchets, beads, and metal pots worth 60 Dutch guilders, or about $1,000 today. The Lenapes had never heard of selling or buying land. They believed that the Europeans would be using the land temporarily.

Forty years later, the British took over the harbor. The Dutch were no match for the British troops, and they surrendered. New Amsterdam became New York.

By the end of the seventeenth century, New York was the fastest growing city in the New World. Goods were shipped between America, England, Africa, and the West Indies. Slave trading was one of the city's most profitable businesses.

In 1776, the Battle of Brooklyn was one of the first major battles of the American Revolution. The British led more than 30,000 soldiers from Staten Island into Brooklyn. After losing 2,000 men in two days, George Washington and his army retreated. The British controlled New York City until the Revolution was won. (School classes can visit the Old Stone House at the site of the Battle of Brooklyn.)

Did You Know?

In 1789, New York City became the first capital of the United States. The capital was moved to Philadelphia in 1791, and ten years later to Washington, D.C.

The city was in ruins after the war, but it was soon rebuilt. New York reestablished itself as a center for trade and manufacturing. The city grew quickly, with the population reaching over 120,000 by 1820.

The Erie Canal was opened in 1825. It connected New York City to the Great Lakes. Goods from the city could be shipped westward, and products from the Midwest could be shipped to New York for export. The city became a great center of international trade.

When the Enrollment Act of 1863 was passed during the Civil War, requiring all men to serve in the army, mobs of angry New Yorkers **rioted**. Some people were also afraid that freed slaves would take their jobs. They set fire to the draft office, stole rifles from an armory, burned down an orphanage for black children, and attacked black people. After four days, hundreds of people had been wounded or killed. The New York City Draft Riots are considered the worst incident of mob violence in American history.

Huge numbers of people **immigrated** to New York City in the middle and late nineteenth century. Irish and Germans, Jewish people from Eastern Europe, French, Russians, and Italians came. They believed New York was a place where they could make a

Federal troops were called in to control angry mobs during the New York City Draft Riots. Before they could restore order, 50 buildings were burned down, and an estimated 120 people were killed and another 2,000 injured. The rioters caused one million dollars worth of damage.

A man checks a cable during the construction of the Empire State Building. About 3,500 workers put in 7 million hours of labor to build the Empire State Building in under 14 months. The frame of the building went up at a rate of one story a day. When it was completed in 1931, the Empire State Building was the tallest skyscraper in the world.

better life for themselves and their families. Most of them arrived through Ellis Island in New York Harbor.

Many immigrants worked in construction, making bridges, railroads, buildings, and streets in New York. Some Americans who had lived there for several generations looked down on the immigrants, but these new Americans built New York into the biggest and most modern city in the world.

In 1898, the five areas called Manhattan, Brooklyn, the Bronx, Queens, and Staten Island were **consolidated**

into New York City. A subway system opened in 1904, letting people who lived outside Manhattan travel to jobs there. The opening of the Brooklyn and Williamsburg bridges, followed soon after by the Manhattan and Queensboro bridges, also helped to connect the five boroughs.

The city now had one public school system. Teachers tried to "Americanize" children as quickly as possible, teaching them English, as well as arithmetic, manners, hygiene, and American history.

By the 1920s, electricity lit up Broadway and the city. People bought automobiles and modern appliances such as vacuum cleaners, telephones, refrigerators, and radios. There were plenty of jobs in making all these goods.

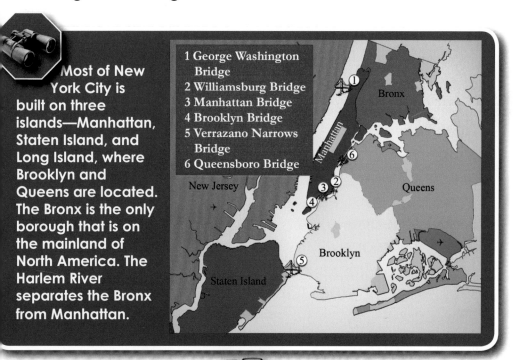

Most of New York City is built on three islands—Manhattan, Staten Island, and Long Island, where Brooklyn and Queens are located. The Bronx is the only borough that is on the mainland of North America. The Harlem River separates the Bronx from Manhattan.

1 George Washington Bridge
2 Williamsburg Bridge
3 Manhattan Bridge
4 Brooklyn Bridge
5 Verrazano Narrows Bridge
6 Queensboro Bridge

Bronx
Manhattan
New Jersey
Queens
Brooklyn
Staten Island

A new type of entertainment emerged in the African-American community of Harlem. White audiences flocked uptown to see plays, jazz music, exotic dancing, and singers. Many African-American writers, poets, artists, and musicians moved to Harlem during this exciting time, known as the Harlem Renaissance. A group of young African-American writers put out a magazine called *Fire!!* Its pages featured works by Langston Hughes, Wallace Thurman, and Zora Neale Hurston, who spoke about what it was like to be black in America. Musicians such as trumpet player Louis Armstrong and singer Billie Holiday lit up nightclub stages.

New York City was also gaining fame as a world financial center. In the early 1900s, many people were buying stocks at the New York Stock Exchange on Wall Street. Stocks are small pieces of ownership of a company. Buyers hoped that the stocks would become more valuable, so they could sell them for a profit. On October 29, 1929, known as Black Tuesday, stock prices fell and the market crashed. Many people lost all the money they had. This was the beginning of the Great Depression.

Louis Armstrong

16

Today, traders at the New York Stock Exchange keep track of the stock market using banks of computers and other hi-tech equipment. A rush to sell stocks like the one in 1929 will trigger the computers to stop trading for the day.

People no longer had money to buy goods, so companies and factories went out of business. People lost their jobs. Hundreds of thousands of New Yorkers were forced to live in the streets or in parks. The Great Depression was one of the worst times in the history of the United States, and New York City was hit especially hard.

During World War II, the **economy** became strong again. In New York, factories were up and running to make equipment for the military. After the war, New York City was the largest manufacturing center, had the largest port, and was the largest financial center in the world. Nearly 1,000 buildings were put up in the ten years after the war. A maze of additional bridges and tunnels connecting Manhattan to the boroughs helped the city grow further.

During the 1960s and '70s, the face of New York City continued to change. Factories closed and were reopened in less expensive buildings. The shipping industry went to New Jersey. Many people moved to the suburbs. Neighborhoods became run down, and people did not have money to pay their rent. In some parts of the city, entire blocks of buildings were abandoned by their owners when they couldn't find renters. Street gangs, drug addicts, and **squatters** moved into the empty buildings. The city nearly became **bankrupt**.

Over the next two decades, the economy of the city improved, and many new businesses opened. Then, on September 11, 2001, the nation's worst disaster occurred. Terrorists **hijacked** two passenger

The Diamond District of midtown Manhattan, along with many other business areas, suffered during the financial crisis of the 1970s. Over 1 million people, and many businesses, left the city. Crime increased, and the city went into decline.

The Twin Towers of Lower Manhattan's World Trade Center, constructed in 1970 and 1971, dominated the New York City skyline until the attacks of September 11, 2001.

planes and crashed them into the Twin Towers of the World Trade Center in Lower Manhattan. The towers collapsed, and several nearby buildings were damaged as well. Nearly 3,000 people died.

In the days and weeks after 9/11, thousands of New Yorkers volunteered to help in every possible way—donating blood, food, and supplies. Doctors volunteered time, restaurant owners made meals for rescue workers, and veterinarians came to help injured rescue dogs.

At first, people were afraid to visit the city, which hurt the economy. Gradually, they started coming again. Some people wanted to see the site of the disaster, **Ground Zero**, but most came because they wanted to be in one of the greatest cities in the world. Construction of a memorial for the September 11 victims began in August 2006.

19

NEW YORK CITY

The Coney Island Cyclone
was declared a National
Historic Landmark in 1991.
Right: A sea turtle at the
New York Aquarium on
Coney Island

The Wild Side of the City

During the last ice age, a huge ice sheet carved out the landforms of New York City. As it melted, it dumped tons of rock, gravel, and dirt in the area. It left behind a land of hills, valleys, and streams.

The Hudson River flows down Manhattan's West Side and separates New York from New Jersey. The East River flows along the East Side of Manhattan. It separates Manhattan from Queens and Brooklyn. The Harlem River separates Manhattan and the Bronx, flowing between the Hudson and East rivers. The East and Hudson rivers flow into New York Harbor, which empties into the Atlantic Ocean.

Coney Island, in Brooklyn, is on the Atlantic Ocean. New Yorkers go there to enjoy summer breezes at the beach and have some fun. Coney Island used to have three amusement parks. In Astroland, the Cyclone, one of the world's oldest and most famous roller coasters, still runs. The New York Aquarium on Surf Avenue has a fabulous collection of marine life. Just outside the aquarium, visitors can have a hot dog

Left: Ice skating at the rink in Rockefeller Center is especially popular during the holidays. Opened on Christmas Day in 1936, over 250,000 skaters enjoy the rink each year, from October to April.

from the original Nathan's—where hot dogs were first made.

New York City has a **humid continental climate**, and four seasons. Winters are cold and bring snow and sleet. On sunny winter days, people can ice skate at Rockefeller Center or in one of the other rinks in the city. Spring and fall are generally pleasant, but summers can be uncomfortably hot and humid, with temperatures in the 80s and 90s. On summer evenings, free concerts are held in some of the many parks throughout the city.

There are more than a dozen types of habitats in New York City, from riverbanks to woods to meadows. The city's natural **ecosystems** provide clean water and air, absorb pollution, and are home to many species, including 3,000 types of plants and more than 350 kinds of birds.

Would you believe that Central Park, right in the middle of Manhattan, is one of the top ten bird-watching sites in the United States? Common city birds such as pigeons and gulls cross paths with shorebirds that include red knots, sandpipers, and plovers. Many migrating songbirds and birds of prey pass through New York City in the spring and fall.

Pale Male and Lola

The most famous bird in New York City is Pale Male, a red-tailed hawk that first appeared around Central Park in the early 1990s. Pale Male and his mate Lola became celebrities when they built their nest on the ledge of a very fancy apartment building on Fifth Avenue. When their nest was removed, local birders and some of the building's famous residents protested. The hawks have since rebuilt their nest on the same building.

Mammals roam the parks and yards of the city, including squirrels, opossum, skunks, raccoons, rabbits, rats, and mice. An increasing number of white-tailed deer live on Staten Island, and even an occasional coyote wanders in from the suburbs.

The saltwater marshes and lagoons of places like Jamaica Bay in Queens provide important habitats for New York City's reptiles and amphibians. Salamanders, frogs, and turtles, including the rare diamondback terrapin, can be spotted. These **estuaries** are also home to mussels, flounder, crabs, and sea urchins. Herons, ibis, and muskrat search them for a meal.

European settlers brought many plants with them, including the grasses they fed to their cattle, herbs used for medicine and cooking, and flowers. By the mid 1800s, 450 plant species, 160 of which had been brought to North America, were recorded in New York City.

Diamondback terrapin

Oak, walnut, cedar, elm, hickory, chestnut, birch, and maple trees were used by the colonists to build houses and furniture. They also burned wood to cook their food and keep their homes warm. Timber was shipped to Europe, because Holland and England had cut down many of their own forests.

When shipbuilding became a major industry in New York City, many trees were felled for this use. Some ended up at the Brooklyn Navy Yard, which the federal government opened more than 200 years ago. During World War II, thousands of workers at the sprawling facility churned out battleships around the clock. Today the yard is a thriving industrial park.

Brooklyn's Prospect Park, Forest Park in Queens, Hunter Island in the Bronx, and the New York Botanical Gardens of the Bronx claim small remnants of the forests that once covered the city. Another break in the concrete of the city is the Bronx Zoo, where visitors can take a safari through sections resembling the Congo, an Asian jungle, and the island of Madagascar.

Glossy ibis

NEW YORK CITY

A view from the upper deck of the old Yankee Stadium, which was used from 1923 to 2008. The new stadium opened in 2009. Right: Lucky Luciano

Chapter **4**

The Many Faces of New York City

New York is run by a mayor, and the city has a history of electing tough, colorful characters, like Fiorello LaGuardia. One of the first things he did as mayor in 1934 was order the chief of police to arrest crime lord Lucky Luciano. Then he went after Luciano's fellow gangsters. "Let's drive the bums out of town," the short, scrappy LaGuardia said during a radio broadcast.

Mayor Ed Koch became known for his refrain to the people: "How'm I doing?" Elected in 1977, he helped clean up the troubled city and make it a more exciting place to live and work during his twelve years in office. Like many of the 104 New York City mayors before him, Koch lived in Gracie Mansion in uptown Manhattan.

The 200-year-old yellow house sits on the edge of Hell Gate, a place in the East River where several waterways tumble into one channel. Hundreds of ships sank there until the late 1800s, when the U.S. Army

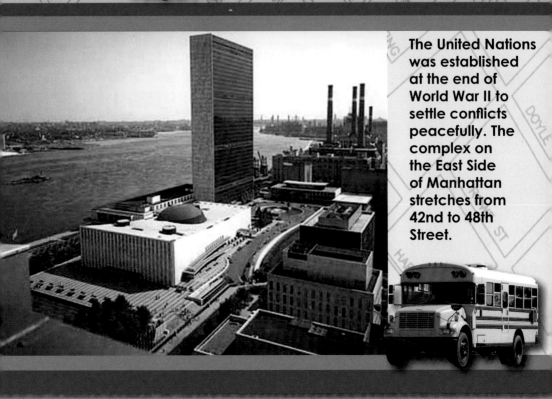

The United Nations was established at the end of World War II to settle conflicts peacefully. The complex on the East Side of Manhattan stretches from 42nd to 48th Street.

Corps of Engineers used 50,000 pounds of explosives to blast the channel's dangerous rocks into bits.

A little farther south, another famous place overlooks the East River. Diplomats from all over the world meet in the United Nations. They talk about ways for countries to work together for peace.

In downtown Manhattan, judges dole out justice at state and city courthouses. Near the southern tip of the island lies the financial district, where stockbrokers wheel and deal on Wall Street.

Throughout all five boroughs of the city are more than 1,400 public schools, teeming with more than a million students. The country's largest public school system also boasts some of the finest. One of them was the model for a television show called *Fame*, about kids who tried out for a high school for the performing arts.

New Yorkers are also proud of their professional sports teams. Baseball fans are loyal to two teams. The Yankees have won twenty-six World Series championships. Until 2008, they played at the legendary Yankee Stadium in the Bronx. Then they moved to a new stadium right next door. The New York Mets, winners of the 1986 World Series, played in Shea Stadium in Queens. In 2009, they moved to Citi Field—also right next door.

Football fans root for the Giants or the Jets. Both teams play in stadiums across the Hudson River in New Jersey. The New York Rangers and the Islanders are New York's National Hockey League teams. The Rangers play in Madison Square Garden in midtown Manhattan; the Islanders play in Nassau Veterans Memorial Coliseum on Long Island. Basketball fans follow the New York Knicks and the Liberty, a professional women's team. Both play at Madison Square Garden, which has arenas that can be switched in just a few hours from

Eli Manning of the NY Giants

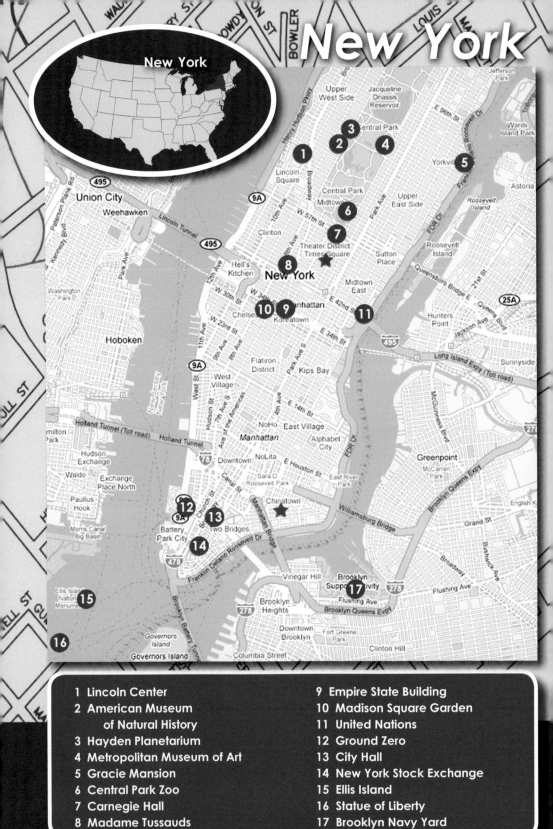

New York

1 Lincoln Center
2 American Museum of Natural History
3 Hayden Planetarium
4 Metropolitan Museum of Art
5 Gracie Mansion
6 Central Park Zoo
7 Carnegie Hall
8 Madame Tussauds
9 Empire State Building
10 Madison Square Garden
11 United Nations
12 Ground Zero
13 City Hall
14 New York Stock Exchange
15 Ellis Island
16 Statue of Liberty
17 Brooklyn Navy Yard

a basketball court to an ice hockey rink to a concert stage.

New Yorkers don't just watch sports—they play them. On spring and fall weekends, the parks are crowded with people kicking soccer balls, throwing Frisbees, rollerblading, and riding bicycles and even horses. In the winter, people ice-skate, bowl, and play tennis and swim indoors. In the summer, kids cool off in the city's more than fifty public swimming pools. Romantic couples rent rowboats for a spin on the Lake in Central Park. More serious boaters can take advantage of the NYC Water Trail, which runs through the five boroughs, connecting 160 square miles of rivers, bays, creeks, inlets, and the Atlantic Ocean.

New York City is an endless source of entertainment. Visitors can enjoy theater on or off Broadway, or go to any of over one hundred museums, from the world-famous Metropolitan Museum of Art to the New York Transit Museum, housed inside a 1930s subway station. Times Square in bustling midtown Manhattan features neon lights, huge billboards, and lots of tourist hotspots. One is Madame Tussauds, with its lifelike wax statues of famous people, from movie stars like Miley Cyrus to historical figures like Benjamin Franklin.

Wax statue of Miley Cyrus at Madame Tussauds

Disney's *Mary Poppins* comes to life on Broadway at the New Amsterdam Theatre. On stage, music and dance entertain audiences of all ages. Many Broadway shows are performed eight times a week, and the actors and dancers give it their all each time.

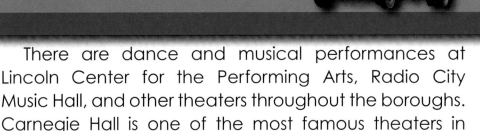

There are dance and musical performances at Lincoln Center for the Performing Arts, Radio City Music Hall, and other theaters throughout the boroughs. Carnegie Hall is one of the most famous theaters in the world.

Eating is another way people "get a taste" of the many cultures in the city. Chinese food in Chinatown, soul food in Harlem, Indian food in the "Little India" of Queens, Latin American food in Sunset Park Brooklyn, and Italian food on Arthur Avenue in the Bronx are just a few of the choices. Several fancy restaurants are perched atop skyscrapers to let diners enjoy beautiful bird's-eye views of the sparkling city.

New York Profiles

Eleanor Roosevelt was born in 1884 in Manhattan. Her uncle was Theodore Roosevelt, the twenty-sixth U.S. president, and she was married to Franklin Delano Roosevelt, the thirty-second president. Eleanor was active in politics both as the First Lady and on her own. She was active in the women's rights and the civil rights movements. Eleanor also wrote a daily newspaper column, *My Day*, and helped found the United Nations.

Fiorello LaGuardia was the mayor of New York City for three terms, from 1934 until 1945. He was one of New York City's most popular mayors. He is fondly remembered for reading the comics to children over the radio during a newspaper strike. Born in Lower Manhattan in 1882, LaGuardia represented the many cultures in the city. His father was Italian, his mother Jewish, and he spoke seven languages. LaGuardia was known as "The Little Flower"—the meaning of his first name. LaGuardia Airport in Queens and Fiorello H. LaGuardia High School of Music & Art and Performing Arts in Manhattan are named for him.

Kareem Abdul-Jabbar is considered to be one of the greatest NBA players of all time. He scored 38,387 points in his career, the highest total of any player in the league's history. He received six MVP (Most Valuable Player) awards. He was born in 1947 in the Inwood section of Manhattan, where he began his basketball career in high school. His thirty-year career in the NBA ended in 1989.

NEW YORK CITY

The Hall of Arms and Armor is one of the most popular exhibits at the Metropolitan Museum of Art on Fifth Avenue. Right: The Alice in Wonderland statue near the Conservatory Water in Central Park

Chapter

5

Our Class Trip to the Big Apple

The day of our trip finally came. We were so excited, we could barely sit still during the bus ride. Luckily, we were able to pass the time by watching a movie called *Home Alone 2: Lost in New York*.

The minute we got there, we broke into two groups. My friend Karl was in the group that toured Central Park, which is right in the middle of Manhattan. Can you believe the park sits on 843 acres of land and has twenty-one playgrounds? There is also a zoo, a lake, two ice rinks, a pool, and even Belvedere Castle, which contains a weather station and a collection of natural history artifacts, like skeletons and old microscopes. The park was designed by Frederick Law Olmsted and built in the 1800s. It was the first **landscaped** public park in the country.

In the afternoon, Karl's group went to the Metropolitan Museum of Art on the east side of the park. In the Egyptian Wing they walked around the stone Temple of Dendur, which was shipped over from Egypt at a cost of about $9.5 million. The Metropolitan also has lots of famous paintings and sculptures, old and new.

Then they went straight across to the west side of the park to the American Museum of Natural History. This museum has one of the largest collections of dinosaur fossils in the world. They ended up watching a space show at the museum's Hayden Planetarium.

Did You Know?
Broadway was once a Lenape hunting trail. The Dutch widened it to make travel easier, and named it *Breed Wegh*.

My group rushed downtown so we wouldn't miss our boat. It took us to two islands. One was Liberty Island, home of the Statue of Liberty, given to the United States by France in 1886. From the top of the statue's ten-story pedestal, we could see boats in New York Harbor and Governor's Island, which is considered to be the birthplace of New York State.

The other island we visited was Ellis Island, where, from 1892 until 1954,

Tyrannosaurus rex fossil in the American Museum of Natural History

The Great Hall on
Ellis Island:
Then (1904) and Now

twelve million immigrants arrived when they reached
America. I got to look up the records of my great
grandfather's boat trip from Austria. Knowing I stood
in the same place he did more than a hundred years
earlier gave me chills.

Back on the bus, we headed to Chinatown, first
settled in the 1800s. It is the largest Chinatown in the
United States. We couldn't wait to order Chinese
food—we were starving! We ate dim sum, little
dumplings, and washed our meal down with tea.

Chinatown's winding, crowded streets also had lots of stores selling Asian toys, foods, fabrics, movies, and video games.

Then we headed to Times Square in Manhattan's theater district. We just had enough time to visit a souvenir shop. I bought some postcards of my favorite sights. Then it was time to see *Mary Poppins*—one of thirty-nine shows running on Broadway that day.

Both groups met up at the Empire State Building on 34th Street. It is 1,472 feet high if you count the antenna at the top. When it was built, it was the tallest building

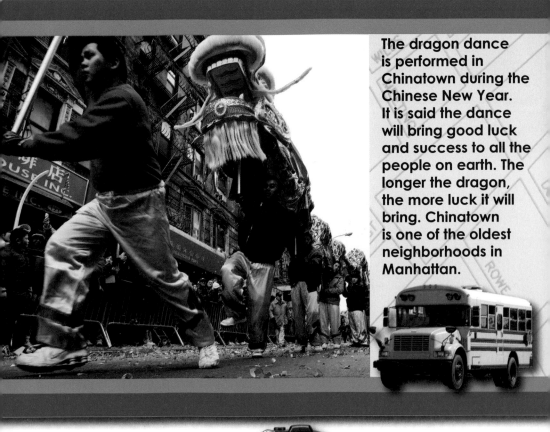

The dragon dance is performed in Chinatown during the Chinese New Year. It is said the dance will bring good luck and success to all the people on earth. The longer the dragon, the more luck it will bring. Chinatown is one of the oldest neighborhoods in Manhattan.

I took a picture from the top of the Empire State Building. You can see its shadow on the shorter buildings below.

in the world. We went to the observatory on the 102nd floor and saw an amazing view of the whole city. People on the streets below looked like tiny ants scurrying around!

Then it was time to head home. I don't think I've ever done so many things in one day before. There are so many more we didn't get to do. I love New York City! I can't wait to go back to New York, New York, which is sometimes called "The Big Apple" or, my favorite, "The city so nice, they named it twice."

Statue of Liberty Torch and Crown

The Statue of Liberty Enlightening the World in New York Harbor is a symbol of freedom and democracy. The seven rays of the crown represent the seven seas and seven continents of the world. The tablet she holds is a book of law, representing justice, and is engraved with the date—July 4, 1776—that the United States declared its freedom from England. At the statue's feet are broken chains, which also symbolize freedom. You can make the statue's crown and torch with simple household items.

MATERIALS:
>   2 sturdy paper plates
>   glue, tape, or staples
>   cardboard paper towel or toilet paper tube
>   gold or yellow tissue paper
>   green paint and paintbrush or a green marker
>   green and gold glitter (optional)

1. Cut out the center of the two paper plates. Save one of the circles you cut out—it will be used to make the rays of the crown. Cut a two-inch piece out of the rims of the paper plates—this will allow the crown to fit on your head. You may need to adjust the size a little.

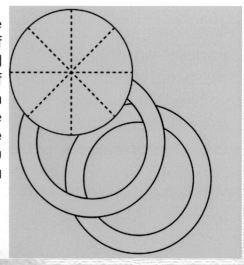

2. Cut the center of one of the plates into eighths by cutting the circle in half, then cutting each half in half, then each quarter in half. You should have 8 triangles. Space 7 of the triangles evenly across the front of one headband and glue or tape them into place to make the seven rays of the Liberty crown. Glue the other rim over the first to hold the ends in place. Paint or color your crown green.

3. Make the torch by painting or coloring a toilet paper or paper towel tube with green paint or marker. Create the flame by crumpling a piece of yellow or gold tissue paper and sticking it into the top of the tube. You could also try cutting the tissue paper into strips, then gluing one end of each strip to the inside of the tube.

4. If you want your crown and torch to really sparkle, decorate them with green and gold glitter.

Just The Facts

Founded: 1624

Location: New York

Form of Government: Mayor

Land Area: 304.8 square miles

Population in 2007: 8.2 Million

U.S. Rank: The most populous city in the U.S.

Density: Approximately 12,350 people per square mile

Average Elevation: 19 feet above sea level

Highest Point: Todt Hill on Staten Island at 409.8 feet

Lowest Point: Sea Level

Average High Temperature: 85°F

Average Low Temperature: 25°F

Hottest Month: July

Coldest Month: January

Hottest Day: July 3, 1966, when a temperature of 107°F was recorded at LaGuardia Airport

Coldest Day: February 9, 1934, when a temperature of −15°F was recorded at LaGuardia Airport

Average Annual Rainfall: 46 inches

Major Industries: Finance, real estate, television and film, advertising, fashion, publishing, the arts, tourism

Latitude: 40° 42' 51" N

Longitude: 74° 0' 23" W

Major Neighborhoods: Manhattan: Downtown, Greenwich Village; East Village, Wall Street, The Lower East Side, Chinatown, Soho, Tribeca, Chelsea, Midtown, Upper West Side and Upper East Side, Harlem **Brooklyn:** Brooklyn Heights, Park Slope, Bay Ridge, Flatbush, Williamsburg, Bedford-Stuyvesant, Canarsie, Bensonhurst, Coney Island **Queens:** Flushing, Astoria, Long Island City, Hunter's Point, Jamaica, Ridgewood, Southern Queens **Bronx:** Riverdale, Van Cortlandt Park, Pelham Bay Park, South Bronx **Staten Island:** St. George, West New Brighton, Emerson Hill, Clifton, Elm Hill, Annadale, Great Kills

Public Parks: Central Park (Manhattan), Prospect Park (Brooklyn); The Greenbelt (Staten Island); Flushing Meadows-Corona Park (Queens); Bronx Park (Bronx)

Major Sports Teams: New York Mets, Yankees—Baseball; New York Knicks—Basketball; New York Islanders, Rangers—Hockey; New York Giants, Jets—Football

Museums and Cultural Centers: American Museum of Natural History, Metropolitan Museum of Art, Museum of Modern Art, Lincoln Center for the Performing Arts (home of The Metropolitan Opera, New York Philharmonic Orchestra, and The New York City Ballet)

*All weather statistics, U.S. National Weather Service, 2007

New York City Historical Timeline

1609   Henry Hudson arrives in New York Harbor.

1624   Dutch build first permanent settlement, named New Amsterdam, on Manhattan Island.

1625   Dutch purchase Manhattan from the Lenapes.

1664   New Amsterdam is conquered by the British, who rename the colony New York.

1776   New York and other colonies declare their independence from England. British troops take over New York City.

1783   British troops leave New York City at the end of the Revolutionary War.

1788   New York becomes the eleventh state.

1789   New York City becomes the country's first capital.

1792   New York Stock Exchange is founded.

1825   Erie Canal opens.

1861–1865   Civil War is fought.

1863   New York City Draft Riots sweep the streets.

1886   France gives the Statue of Liberty to United States.

1898   Five boroughs are consolidated into New York City.

1914–1919   World War I is fought.

1929   The Stock Market Crash ushers in the Great Depression.

1939–1945   World War II is fought.

1950   United Nations opens in Manhattan.

2001   World Trade Center is attacked on September 11.

2009   Two brand-new baseball stadiums—Yankee Stadium and Citi Field—open in time for Major League Baseball's opening day.

Glossary

bankrupt (BANK-rupt)—Out of money.

borough (BUR-oh)—One of the five political divisions of New York City.

consolidated (kun-SAH-lih-day-ted)—Brought parts together into one.

Dutch West India Company—A large trading company that operated out of the Netherlands in the 1600s.

economy (ee-KAH-nuh-mee)—The exchange of goods and money.

ecosystems (EE-koh-sis-tums)—Collections of living things and their environment.

estuaries (ES-choo-wayr-ees)—Areas where freshwater meets salt water.

First Lady—The wife of the United States president.

Ground Zero—The area where the World Trade Center towers once stood.

hijacked (HY-jakd)—Taken and forced to go to another place.

humid continental climate—Climate marked by variable weather patterns and large differences in seasonal temperatures.

immigrated (IH-mih-gray-ted)—Moved into a country from another.

landscaped (LAND-skaypt)—Planted with trees and flowers to make more attractive.

Lenape (leh-NAH-pay)—One of the Native American tribes of the Mid-Atlantic and Northeastern states.

Northwest Passage—A ship route along the Arctic coast of Canada and Alaska, joining the Atlantic and Pacific oceans.

rioted (RY-ah-ted)—Took part in a violent public disturbance.

squatters (SKWAH-ters)—People who move into abandoned buildings and use them as a home.

Further Reading

Books

Conway, Lorie. *Forgotten Ellis Island: The Extraordinary Story of America's Immigrant Hospital.* New York: Smithsonian Books/Collins, 2007.

Fischer, Laura. *Life in New Amsterdam.* Chicago: Heinemann Library, 2003.

Greene, Jacqueline Dembar. *The 2001 World Trade Center Attack (Code Red).* New York: Bearport Publishing, 2007.

Hopkinson, Deborah. *Sky Boys: How They Built the Empire State Building.* New York: Random House, 2006.

Konigsburg, E. L. *From the Mixed-Up Files of Mrs. Basil E. Frankweiler.* New York: Aladdin, 2007.

Ogintz, Eileen. *The Kid's Guide to New York City.* Guilford, Conn.: Globe Pequot Press, 2004.

Schulman, Janet. *Pale Male: Citizen Hawk of New York City.* New York: Knopf Books for Young Readers, 2008.

Internet Sources

Day in the City: New York
http://www.nickjr.com/travel/gck_day_in_the_city/gck_ditc_new_york/index.jhtml

Empire State Building, Official Internet Site
http://www.esbny.com/kids

New York City Audubon, Look Around NYC
http://www.nycaudubon.org/kids/lanyc/

On-Lion for Kids!, New York, New York!
http://kids.nypl.org/newyork/index.cfm

Pale Male
http://www.palemale.org

PBS Kids Go!, Big Apple History
http://pbskids.org/bigapplehistory/index-flash.html

Works Consulted

Burns, Ric, and James Sanders. *New York: An Illustrated History*. New York: Alfred A. Knopf, 2003.

Burrows, Edwin G., and Mike Wallace. *Gotham: A History of New York City to 1898*. New York: Oxford University Press, 1999.

Hayes, William. *City in Time: New York*. New York: Sterling Publishing, 2007.

Homberger, Eric. *New York City: A Cultural History*. Northampton, Mass.: Interlink Books, 2008.

Marshall, Bruce. *Building New York: The Rise and Rise of the Greatest City on Earth*. New York: Universe Publishing, 2005.

Quigley, David. *Second Founding: New York City, Reconstruction, and the Making of American Democracy*. New York: Farrar, Straus and Giroux, 2004.

Shorto, Russell. *The Island at the Center of the World*. New York: Vintage, 2005.

Trager, James. *The New York Chronology*. New York: HarperCollins, 2003.

Exploring the Nature of New York
    http://www.ive.cuny.edu/nynn/home.htm
Official New York City Government Website
    www.nyc.gov
Official Tourism Website of New York City
    http://nycvisit.com/
Old Stone House, Brooklyn
    http://www.theoldstonehouse.org/
Overview of New York Geology
    http://gretchen.geo.rpi.edu/roecker/nys/nys_edu.pamphlet.html
Statue of Liberty/Ellis Island Foundation
    http://www.ellisisland.org/
Wildlife Conservation Society—The Mannahatta Project
    http://www.wcs.org/

Index

ABOUT THE AUTHOR

Elizabeth Scholl has written numerous social studies books and magazine articles for children, teachers, and parents. She was born and raised in the borough of Queens, in New York City. She attended New York University in Manhattan. For fifteen years, Elizabeth lived and taught elementary school in Brooklyn and Manhattan. She currently lives in Bergen County, New Jersey, a suburb of New York City, with her husband, three children, one very large dog, and two orange cats. When not writing, she enjoys gardening, reading, bicycling, and going to New York City with her family to see museums, historic sites, concerts, and other cool stuff.

DISARD